Pebble® Plus

All about Spring

Animals in Spring

by Martha E. H. Rustad

Consulting Editor: Gail Saunders-Smith, PhD

Consultant: John D. Krenz, PhD
Department of Biological Sciences
Minnesota State University, Mankato

CAPSTONE PRESS
a capstone imprint

Pebble Plus is published by Capstone Press,
1710 Roe Crest Drive, North Mankato, Minnesota 56003.
www.capstonepub.com

Library of Congress Cataloging-in-Publication Data
Rustad, Martha E. H. (Martha Elizabeth Hillman), 1975-
Animals in spring / by Martha E. H. Rustad.
    p. cm. — (Pebble plus: all about spring)
ISBN 978-1-4296-8655-6 (library binding)
ISBN 978-1-4296-9358-5 (paperback)
ISBN 978-1-62065-286-2 (ebook PDF)
1. Spring—Juvenile literature. 2. Animals—Juvenile literature. I. Title.

QB637.5.R867 2012
591.5—dc23   2012000125

Editorial Credits
Shelly Lyons, editor; Bobbie Nuytten, designer; Svetlana Zhurkin, photo researcher;
    Kathy McColley, production specialist

Photo Credits
Alamy: Don Johnston, 12–13; Dreamstime: Lori0469, 18–19, Omers, 14–15, Peter Clark, 20–21, Roberto222, 8–9;
iStockphoto: Steve Greer, 4–5; Shutterstock: irin-k, 1, 16–17, Kane513, 6–7, Marish (green leaf), cover and throughout,
Matthew Williams-Ellis, cover, Steve Byland, 10–11, Zubada (leaf pattern), cover

Note to Parents and Teachers

The All about Spring series supports national science and social studies standards related to changes during the seasons. This book describes and illustrates animals in spring. The images support early readers in understanding the text. The repetition of words and phrases helps early readers learn new words. This book also introduces early readers to subject-specific vocabulary words, which are defined in the Glossary section. Early readers may need assistance to read some words and to use the Table of Contents, Glossary, Read More, Internet Sites, and Index sections of the book.

Printed in the United States   5029

Table of Contents

Springtime

Spring is here!
Animals are active
in the warmer weather.

Waking Up

Black bears come out of dens.

They sniff for new plants

and animals to eat.

Honeybees leave the hive.

They buzz near blooming flowers.

They gather nectar and pollen.

Frogs croak and call
to find mates.

Coming Home

Monarch butterflies travel north.
They rest and lay eggs
on milkweed leaves.

Sandhill cranes fly
thousands of miles.
Flocks gather
at melting ponds.

New Life

Ducklings hatch from eggs.
They waddle
across the grass.

Fox kits play.

Their mother stays nearby.

She feeds her kits milk.

In spring, animals find food.

Young animals explore.

What changes do you see

in spring?

Glossary

bloom—to flower

den—a place where a wild animal may live

explore—to go searching or looking around

hatch—to break out of an egg

hive—a place where many bees live; thousands of bees live in one hive

kit—a young fox; female foxes can have four to nine kits at one time

mate—a male or female partner of a pair of animals

nectar—a sweet liquid that some insects collect from flowers and eat as food

pollen—tiny, yellow grains in flowers; some insects eat pollen

waddle—to walk with short steps and a swaying motion

22

Read More

Berger, Melvin and Gilda. *A Robin Grows Up.* Now I Know. New York: Scholastic, 2008.

Esbaum, Jill. *Everything Spring.* Washington, D.C.: National Geographic, 2010.

Smith, Siân. *Spring.* Seasons. Chicago: Heinemann Library, 2009.

Internet Sites

FactHound offers a safe, fun way to find Internet sites related to this book. All of the sites on FactHound have been researched by our staff.

Here's all you do:

Visit *www.facthound.com*

Type in this code: 9781429686556

 Super-cool stuff! Check out projects, games and lots more at www.capstonekids.com

23

Index

Word Count: 105
Grade: 1
Early-Intervention Level: 13